# SILVERSMITHING FOR

# BEGINNERS

Practical Guide with Tips, Techniques, and Projects for Jewelry Makers.

**Connor Howard**

**Revised Edition 2023**

# TABLE OF CONTENTS

# CHAPTER ONE

## INTRODUCTION TO SILVERSMITHING

Silversmithing is the process of crafting Jewelry from silver or sterling. It involves forming and working with silver to create ornamental pieces, Jewelry, armor, vases, and decorative valuables.

In the past, "goldsmithing" and "silversmithing" were synonymous. Both professions were together until silver gained in popularity and social acceptance. Below are the steps involved in jewelry silversmithing, which could be used as the overall technique.

### ➤ Cutting or Sawing the Metal

If you are working with a metal wire, you need wire cutters to cut the average size length. But when using flat sheets of metals, a jewelry maker will use unique Jewelry saw to cut out shapes or strips for making a piece of Jewelry.

### ➤ Filing the Metal

As soon as the metal is cut, a jeweler's file is used to file down the rough edges before the actual shaping and soldering. Filing can also be done later on after soldering is done. Jeweler's files are of various sizes, and you need 0 or 1 size for heavy filing.

## ➢ Shaping and Hammering (The Metal Work)

The best time to shape silver metal is when it's cold. Now, you can hammer, texture, and bend it into shape with a rawhide jeweler's hammer.

## ➢ Soldering

You have to use Solder to fix two pieces of metal together. For instance, to link a ring band or add more light to a piece. A solution referred to as "pickle" is used to clean the shaped metal in an acidic solution. After this, "Flux" will treat the metal, ensuring it is clean while heated and allows the Solder to flow. It must be heated at the appropriate temperature before it can be soldered. As a beginner, this can be tricky to ascertain the right temperature, but a general rule of thumb is to make sure that the metal is showing red before adding the Solder to link the metal together. The metal is to be cleaned again using the "pickle" solution for some minutes after the soldering process.

## ➢ Finishing and Polishing

Finishing a piece of silver Jewelry requires it to be polished to obtain a shiny and smooth surface. To achieve this, use a buffing wheel, a piece of cloth, and rough jeweler's polish as the finishing step. Other finishing at this stage could include but are not limited to an antique or patina silver finish.

# CHAPTER TWO

## TOOLS FOR MAKING SILVERSMITHING

## JEWELRY

A few vital tools are needed in this discipline to complete various projects. However, sophisticated tools are also available to boost your skills and produce a more crafted-looking final stage product. Most of these tools are very easy for silversmiths, and those who find hobbies are all life skills. Below is a list of silversmithing tools and the importance or uses of each.

## 1. Scissors & Snicks

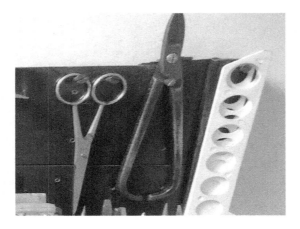

Snicks look more like little scissors, and they come in various sizes of handles to match your personal preference and needs. Silversmith Snicks is extensively used in Jewelry, its cuts little metal pieces easily. I recommend this tool for silversmiths in all skills, especially when working with small pieces of silver.

## 2. Cutters & Pliers

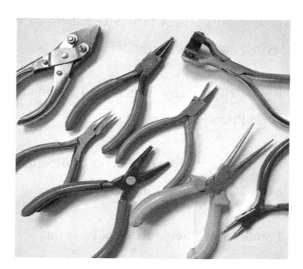

I. Flush Cutters

Flush cutters are essential for cutting your silver wire without much stress. With it, the filing steps are much more comfortable. Whenever wire solders are used, it cuts them perfectly well. Below are a few examples of flush cutters that performs very well, especially on wire solder, which are always available on Amazon.

- Hakko Microsoft Flush Cutters

- Xuron Micro-Shear Flush Cutters

II. Pliers

Also available on Amazon are different varieties of pliers that serve multiple purposes. Crafters use them in wire wrapping and wire weaving, and silversmiths.

- Round Nose Pliers (check out Pandahall Ergonomic Round Nose Pliers on Amazon)

- Needle Nose Pliers (check out Professional High Quality 6" Mini Needle Nose Pliers on Amazon)

- Parallel Jaw Pliers (also available on Amazon is Mazbot Smooth Flat Jaw Parallel Pliers)

3. Jeweler's Saw

Another name for the jeweler's saw is "piercing saw"; this saw is one of the standard tools always seen in a jeweler's craft shop. I usually work on silver metals; it is excellent to cut pieces of metal into unique sizes and shapes. This saw comes with adjustable blades based on your application interest. This tool is essential to diverse kinds of silversmiths.

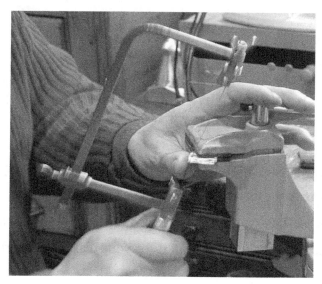

4. Jeweler's Files

The jeweler's files look exactly like those used in filing daggers, knives, and other shaped objects. The jeweler's files are available for use in jewelry and
silversmithing trades. The files feature round, half-round, and flat shapes; I make curves or grooves into workpieces with rounded files and smoothened out specific parts.

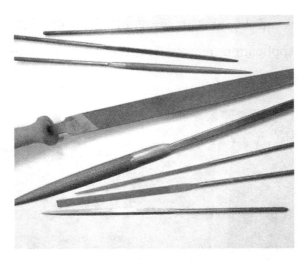

The flat flies are multi-purpose in nature. Hence they are versatile tools used in many different silver working projects. The size and types of flats you need depend solely on your application interest. These files would be essential for your reasonable periods.

5. Jeweler's Anvil

The anvil is undoubtedly one of the most vital pieces that should be readily available in any metalworker's craft shop. With anvils, you can make stable, firm surfaces where you can work and craft metals in various forms or other complex objects without thinking of breakages.

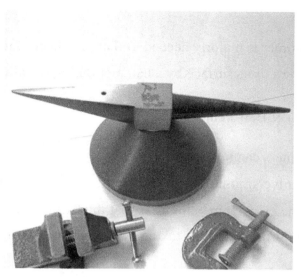

The anvil comes with little features with a pritchel hole, which is necessary to shape Jewelry and permit you to mold the particular piece of work quickly.

6. Planishing Hammer

Planishing hammer is majorly needed to flatten a sheet of metal via continuous blows to its surface by a hammer during metalworking.

7.  Cross-Pein & Ball-Pein hammer

Ball-pein hammers can be used in various ways, including jewelry-making and silversmithing. The only difference between this hammer and the cross-pein hammer is that the ball pein hammer is round-headed, forming hollow, textured shapes into sheet metal.

The cross-pein hammer comes with a round flat head and thin edge that creates textured markings on metal surfaces. This hammer is essential in making jewelry and silversmithing projects.

8.  Stakes

Stakes are essential tools used when forming silver into different shapes. They come in diverse shapes to reshape different designs.

9.  Polishing & Sanding Tools

There are various kinds of hand-held and rotating tools used for silversmithing. The tools cover brushes, simple buffs, and sanding tools. Buffs are used to create a lustrous finish on the surface of the workpiece.

Wire brushes are very active in smoothening and polishing rough surfaces because their abrasive characteristics can erase many materials.

To obtain a more unison finish with the highest accuracy, rotating heads such as bands, abrasive wheels, and polishing bristles.

## 10. Bench Vise

Bench vise holds the workpiece in place while the metalworker shapes it without applying their hands.

## 11. Torch

One essential tool to have when working with metals is a torch. During formation and shaping, it eases your effort to work it as a smith.

## 12. Pickle

This liquid is always heated before it's used to promote performance. It is sediment before and after the soldering process, erases flux, and all other oxidation seen on soldered metals.

# CHAPTER THREE

## MATERIALS AND SUPPLIES: MAKING THE RIGHT CHOICE

This chapter has covered the essential materials and supplies you need for silversmithing

**1. Silver Wire**

A silver wire could be half-round or round, whichever you prefer, or maybe both.

I.  Half Round

If you wish to make a ring, go for half-round silver wire. You can get it from a craft store, such as 10g Half Round Sterling Silver Wire or 20g Half Round Sterling Silver Wire.

II. Round Wire

Round wire is a perfect choice for additional comfort while producing rings. (You can check out Sterling Silver Round Wire, Gauge 2g to 30g at the Rio Grande, and 20g Sterling Silver Round Wire on Amazon).

## 2. Solder

Solders come in diverse forms; the choice is left to you to decide which to adopt. The project you embark on will determine whether you will go for easy, medium, or hard solders. There are also other options like extra each and extra hard densities. It all depends on your particular project. Silver wire solders are available at Rio Grande and Amazon.

**Wire**

- 20g Silver Wire Solder 3ft (check out Easy, Medium, or Hard on Amazon)

- 22g Silver Wire Solder (see Easy, Medium, or Hard at the Rio Grande). The preferred choice of Solder.

**Sheet**

- 28g Silver Sheet Solder Kit, 1DT (check out each of Easy, Medium, and Hard on Amazon)

- 30g Silver Sheet Solder (check out Easy, Medium, and Hard on the Rio Grande)

**Chips**

Chips are known as a sheet and wire solder unless it has been pre-cut into smaller pallets. Many jewelers prefer the sheet and wire solder because it allows them to customize what they like, but I will still list other options for you,

- 20ip Solder, 1,000 pieces (check out in Amazon Easy, Medium, and Hard)

- 30g Silver Chip Solder (check out at Rio Grande Easy, Medium, and Hard).

**Paste**

Paste also contains flux inside it; hence it is a 2-in-1 product. I love it because it brings the perfect result to my work. You can purchase 1DT Silver Paste Solder at Rio Grande.

## 3. Flux

With flux, your metal is protected from fire scale and allows your Solder to move smoothly.

- 1quarter My-T Flux (check out on Rio Grande)

- 80z Handy flux (available on Amazon)

## 4. Polishing

You would wish to polish your work at the end of your project. You can adopt various ways to polish your work, but since we are talking about materials and supplies, it will come up much later, though little has been discussed in cap one above.

- Sunshine Polishing Cloths, 7.74 by 5"(3), are available on Amazon; these are the best. You may consider other options: Tumbler, Dremel, or Flex Shaft coupled with a felt polishing tip and a red rough polishing compound.

## 5. Mask

Masking is vital while working on your project. With this, it helps to prevent fumes inhalation coming from soldering or polishing a piece. These masks come in various forms, but I recommend the one I use most often.

- 3M Particulate Filter (2) 2096 P100 on Amazon

- 3M Half Mask Respirators on Amazon, you can find them in Small, Medium, and Large.

# CHAPTER FOUR

## SILVERSMITHING JEWELRY MAKING
## TOOLS AND SUPPLIES AT A GLANCE

Here are vital jewelry-making tools and supplies. Some have been mentioned earlier, but the purpose of this chapter is to bring you the vital tools and supplies at a glance without stress. They range from wire cutters, pliers, jeweler's saws, hammers, bench blocks, drills (both manual and power-driven), hole punches, classic wire working, stringing, beading, and kumihimo tools.

This supplies section includes work lamps, magnifiers, measuring gauges, safety glasses, antiquing solutions, polishers, jewelry cleaners, storage organizers, adhesives, and specialty magnets.

1. Safety Gear and Safety Glasses

2. Accessories and Flex-Shaft System

3. Steel Shot and Tumblers

4. Wire Cutters and Jewelry Pliers

5. Supplies and Riveting Tools

6. Leather Pads and Rubber Bench Blocks

7. Draw Plates

8. Jewel Setting Tools

9. Loupes and Magnifiers

10. Work Lamps

11. Jewelry Glues and Adhesives

12. Stringing Tools and Beading

13. Antiquing Solutions and Oxidizers

14. Firing Supplies, Kilns, and Torches

15. Bracelet Tools

16. Metal Clay Tools

17. Spring Bar Removal

18. Embossing Tools, Big Shot, and BIGkick

19. Tassel Maker Tools

20. Jewelry Screwdrivers and Watch

21. Mandrels

22. Gauges and Calipers

23. Ring-Making Supplies

24. Organizers and Jewelry Supply Storage

25. Bulk Magnet

26. Polishers and Cleaners

27. Tools Kits and Tools Sets

28. Books and Wire Working Tools

29. Engraving Supplies and Etching

30. Supplies and Jewelry Soldering Tools

31. Accessories and Benchtop Polisher

32. Burnisher

33. More Metalworking Tools

34. Glues and Leather Jewelry-Making Tools

# CHAPTER FIVE

## TECHNIQUES (BASIC, SURFACE, SPECIALIST)

There are only five jewelry silversmithing techniques, from the design you have in mind to the necklace on your neck or whatever piece of Jewelry you wish to craft. Most silver jewelry-making projects don't even need all six techniques. Breaking down silversmithing into manageable steps and methods and practicing them one after the other, I realized that making custom silver jewelry is an achievable process that brings fun to the crafter.

Below are the six techniques you could go through for a successful silversmithing project.

**1. Cutting or Sawing the metal**

- The metal you desire to cut should be placed over the "V" of your wooden bench pin, ensuring you press it down firmly.

- Grip the saw's frame slightly while your body and arm are relaxed.

- Use beeswax to lubricate your saw blade.

- Place your safety glasses on always.

- The saw should be slightly angled, lowering the blade with long, even strokes until the first cut is achieved.

- The saw should be moved back to a vertical position and kept cutting, ensuring you cut on the wrong side of your design, going up and down in your movement.

- Whenever you are to cut curves or turn corners, the metal should be moved instead of the saw. It ensures minimal broken blades and maximal control over the cutting.

**More Tips:**

- Protective finger tape should be wrapped within your thumb and first finger to guide your nails and fingers during cutting.

- Keep the pressure on the upstroke minimal; cutting only occurs on the downstroke.

- There should be various saw blades with different grades of blades around you to avoid changing blades over and over.

As you saw with long strokes, use the blade's complete length, applying slight pressure.

- If you wish to cut from the center of the metal, bore a hole with the help of an HSS drill bit or open a spot using a central tool, after which input your blade into the hole.

## 2. Filing the Metal

One of the jewelers' basic techniques is filling because the file ranks highest among vital shaping and finishing tools. Files can be used for shaping, cutting, and smoothening metals. The following are the basic filling techniques adopted by various silversmiths.

-        Outward Curves: As soon as the file moves forward, your wrist should be bent slightly and your elbow lifted to follow the surface elevation. The file should move in a smooth continuous curve as you apply long strokes, or else you will experience flat spots on the Jewelry.

-        Inward Curves: You will need to use a file with a rounded face to enable you to file an outward curve. An oval, half-round, round, or crossing file can be used. As you push forward, the file should be allowed to roll from one side to another. It eliminates cutting irregular flat spots on the edge of the metal.

-        Flat Filing: The work should be steady when filing straight lines or flat surfaces. Only the file should move.

**More Tips:**

-        Extra care should be taken so that you do not remove excess metal. As any metal removed can't be replaced.

-        It would be best if you stopped filing when you notice the Solder's outline is barely visible. The remaining Solder will be removed during sanding to prepare the metal for polishing. Filing to remove all Solder will make the metal thinner than necessary, especially during sanding.

## 3. Shaping and Hammering (The Metal Work)

-        The best time to shape and hammer a silver metal is when it is cold. A rawhide jeweler's hammer can be beaten, textured, and bent into different shapes and sizes.

-       Many different types of Hammers abound. You can shape a silver metal within a ring, neck mandrel, or bracelet to create the needed curves, or better still, hammer and texture on a flat metal block.

## 4. Soldering

Firstly, the solder area needs to be safe. You may use a large ceramic tile, a fire brick or heat resistance pad, and an overhead lamp. Place the fire brick on top of the tile. Ensure your working area is well-ventilated. Before soldering, you may desire to keep the following items nearby: a jar of water, a small paintbrush, a pair of copper tongs, your Solder, a pocket pot, and flux.

- Preparing the Metal: Ensure your metal is clean and free from grease, oil, and all dirt that may have come in contact with the metal through hand touching. Every piece to be soldered should be placed into a pickle for some minutes. As soon as they are out of the pickle, use a pair of tweezers or pliers, handle the metal, and place it on the fire brick in readiness for soldering.

The addition of Flux: At this time, you use very shape scissors or a wire cutter to cut out little pieces of Solder. Keep them apart on your tile for later use. There are two different ways and kinds of flux. It is now a matter of choice, but you can do any of the following:

I.      This type uses the flux called Battens. The color is light yellow. A thin paintbrush is used to apply the flux to the area ready to be soldered. Then the Solder will be placed on the metal. By this, the Solder and flux are heated together simultaneously.

II.     The second type uses a flux called Borax, which is more like a paste. It is still applied using a thin brush. However, the Solder is not applied immediately, but the metal will first be heated until the fluxed area looks more like glass. After which, the Solder is placed on the metal.

-       Positioning the Solder: Placing the tiny pieces of Solder onto the metal works well with tweezers. Use the area that will join very well to the metal to place the Solder. Applying a small amount of Solder will be fine if adequately placed. Unfortunately, without practice, this seems almost impossible.

-       Torch it: As soon as your Solder is in place, the time is ripe for torching. Heat all the metal to arrive at the soldering temperature simultaneously. Ensure you do not point the flame right at the Solder because the Solder will follow the heat.

Keep on the flame until you see the solder run; remove the flame quickly.

-       Quenching the Metal: With your plier or tweezer, collect the hot metal and drop it into the jar of water close to you, as earlier stated. To sell the piece again, you must go through these steps. As previously stated, you may change a different kind of Solder, either soft or medium.

**More Tips:**

-       Turn on your Crock-Pot of pickle solution (pH Down and water) when you start a workday at your bench or a silversmithing project;

-       Then the pickle should be hot and ready to clean your silver jewelry projects when you are set for it;

-       Pickle cleanses pieces of silver Jewelry before and after soldering.

**5. Finishing**

There are different types of finishing: Brushed, Satin(matte) (although many consider these to mean the same thing), Etched, Plated, Sandblast, Patina and High Polish (or other finish), and so on. Jewelry doesn't have to be shiny always; in fact, many like me prefer not to have a high shine.

-       Finishing around a stone, use tape to protect the stone, a finger, or anything that works for you. The abrasive compounds used can affect the shape and shine of your stone.

-       If you damage the shine on your stone, you can apply a combination of fine sanding papers and diamond paste to correct and bring back the luster or eliminate scratches. You can find Diamond paste in many different grits. I prefer using felt buff, a teeny bit of water, and my flex shaft to bring back the shine to a stone.

## 6. Three Basic Polishing Techniques

I.      Split Lapping/Rough Cut: This process eliminates sharp edges, scratches, and burns quickly. It is a very aggressive, abrasive metal eliminator. Preferably use Tripoli.

II.     Polishing: If all-atom of the filing or sanding marks are eliminated, it will produce a "dull" finish. You can use Tripoli or Bobbing compounds, which lead to moderate metal removal. And at this time, the surface is refined. Polishing is best suitable for abrasive belts or discs. Once polishing is done, you can proceed to buff.

III.    Buffing makes use of compounds and fabric wheels. The roughest cutting compound can remove marks left by 320-400 abrasive grit.

**More Tips on Buffing Wheel:**

-       The work is not done by the buff but by the compound.

-       Every compound should have a separate buff; the compound and buff used should be kept in a one-labeled bag. Mixing up your compounds on the same wheel will lead to a very confused wheel, and the compound won't act accordingly.

-       If your buffs are dirty or "thread," you can use a regular 'ole folk to clean them up.

-       Bits of metal debris, dirt, and other flotsam and jetsom can lead to deep scratches. Cleaning with ultrasound cleaner or scrubbing with a brush and soapy water can remove all remaining investment on cast pieces.

# CHAPTER SIX

## SOME INSPIRING STEP-BY-STEP PROJECTS

Simple Silver Ring Band

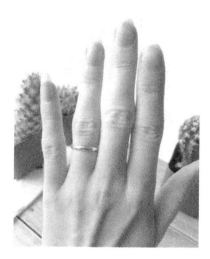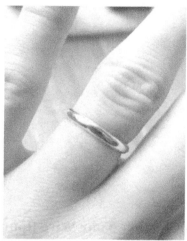

### Step 1: Selecting the Right Wire

The most popular choice of wire I used in making this simple silver ring band is the half-round wire or round wire.

### Step 2: Take Your Wire Measurement

I'm opting for a five-ring band to take my sharpie and Mark it at 2".

You can cut your wire in many ways, first. You can create your round ring.

Then, at the spot where your wire overlaps, use your saw and saw to make an excellent flush cut with little to no filing required.

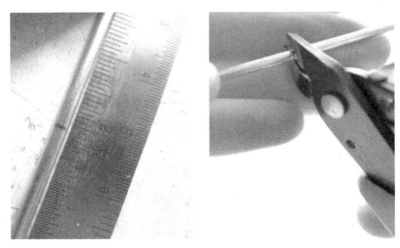

**Step 3: Make Your Wire Round**

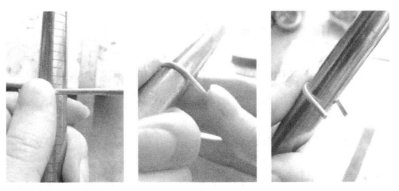

With your steel ring mandrel, start wrapping your wire within it.

Since I'm making a five-size ring band, I'm wrapping my mandrel at a size 4, so it evens; I hope that makes sense.

As soon as you get all the wire rounds, you will notice that the ends will be hard to push down. It is where you will apply your rawhide mallet.

Each end of the wire is expected to be hammered to ensure a complete circle.

**Step 4: Flatten Up Your Ring**

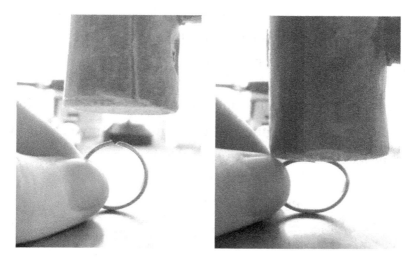

What you will do next is to flatten your ring to a level where the two ends join parallel.

It is easier to file the ends flat, after which you solder using the most contact of the ends.

Hold your ring upon your anvil and hammer until it obtains a flat edge.

**Step 5: Filing Your Ends Flat**

It is the hardest part of this work, in my opinion.

Be very careful when pushing the ends together so there is no gap in between.

The Solder will not fill any gap in between, so if there is a gap, it will give a weak gap and finally leads to a break.

You can file your ends in many different ways, but I like filling mine this way, clamping the end of my ring with my parallel jaw pliers just a tad.

Ensure Your end is perpendicular to your pliers.

Hold your pliers up against your bench pin and file until there is no more metal sticking up further than your pliers, then look at your file line, then file some more if required, then look again, so ensure you file flat and not at an angle.

As soon as you notice both ends are perfectly flat, begin to twist and turn every end through every other so that your ring stays close using tension.

Now hold it up to a light; if you notice a light coming through, you need to open it back up and file again.

As you hold it up, you will observe which end needs filing.

Immediately, your ends are flat; you will hold each end, using your hands or tools, then twist into the opposite side to create tension, do this for some time, then line up each end so they match up and let go.

**Step 6: Solder Your Ring Shut**

Use your flux, most times with Handy flux; add some water to it, preferably distilled, to produce moisture because it gets dry for some reason, even as the lid is on.

So stir it up; I like to use a scrap copper wire to apply the flux to the seam, but using a toothpick will be fine, or the special brush reserved for applying flux, a flux brush.

Ensure you flux the seam all around.

Then Snick out a bit of pallien of Solder; I prefer using hard Solder.

The Solder can be applied in many different ways. It all depends on the project in question.

Solder flux in the heat direction; I will heat the ring a little by moving it in a circular motion.

It is one of the great ways to solder because the little solder pieces will raise your once placed underneath, then you will observe the ring plop down to your soldering board as soon as the Solder has flowed.

Once you are done, use your Jewelers Weezer to place your ring into your glass of water, then test your link by pulling on it to ensure it's an excellent solder link.

## Step 7: Pickle Up Your Ring

Mix your pickle solution with a cup of white vinegar per 1 generous tablespoon salt.

Pour it into your Crock-Pot; up to just about an inch is good.

Please put on your Crock-Pot, raise it high to about 180°F, and let it warm up.

As soon as you notice condensation under your lid, plop in your ring.

Allow it to rest for about 10 minutes.

Only use copper, bamboo, or plastic tong to bring out your ring when you're done.

### Step 8: Form Your Ring

You will use your ring mandrel and rawhide mallet in this step.

Slide your ring over your mandrel and pull it down as much as possible.

Use your mallet and begin to hammer out the lumps and bumps.

Use your other hand to slide it down and hammer it.

As soon as you get the bumps, take off the ring, flip it over, and hammer it again to prevent it from getting tempered slightly.

## Step 9: Time to Polish Your Ring

Take 1 In of stainless steel shot and pour it into your barrel.

Then, fill it with water just about 1/4" above the shot.

Pour in some drops of your burnishing compound.

I'm using the Super Sunsheen from the Rio Grande.

You may use blue Dawn dish soap instead of the burnishing compound.

Place your lid on and allow it to tumble for about 1 hour. As soon as you have this, you are done.

## Bamboo Stacking Rings

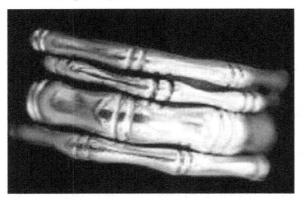

Step 1

Draw a circle with the help of a compass on graph paper, a little bit smaller than the diameter in your ring.

Divide the circle into eight cardinal points: North, South, East, West, North East, South East, etc.

Step 2

Place your ring on the circle drawn. At point North, create a vertical line on the ring.

With a saw blade 2/0 score that lines entirely around the ring stock.

Rotate the ring a quarter turn so that the last line scored will be facing East.

At the North point, scribe and score.

Turn to another quarter and scribe/score again on the North Pole.

Repeat this process to divide the ring into four equal parts.

Step 3

Place your ring again on the paper template.

Between the North and the East, scribe a line.

With a saw blade of 2/0, a score that lines around the shank.

Choose North-East as the new scribing and scoring point, rotate the ring facing South-East, then repeat.

Continue doing that until the ring is wholly divided into eight equal parts.

Step 4

Measure one millimeter to the right of every scored line, and then scribe a second line with a saw blade of 2/0 score all around the shank.

The second line should taper towards the ring's center point and not exactly parallel to the other.

Step 5

With a triangular file, cut V-shape grooves in each scored line.

To round the sides of the V grooves, use the crossing file.

Step 6

To make the curved bamboo shape, make use of the crossing file.

From the center of every segment, file a shallow U-shape into it. It should be done in all eight sections.

Repeat the process on both sides of the ring to taper every segment around the shank.

Step 7

The flex shaft handpiece should be fastened into the vise.

Rough out the rest of the bamboo shape with a silicone wheel.

The marks should be smoothened using the BLUE silicone wheel.

Then, the characters should be further smoothened using the PINK silicone wheel.

Step 8

The ring will be finished with a muslin wheel loaded with Zip finishing gouge or polish.

Your Bamboo Stacking Rings are ready.

Silver Ball and Wire Decorated Ring

Step 1: Measure the Size

Ensure the length of the four silver wires is the same length.

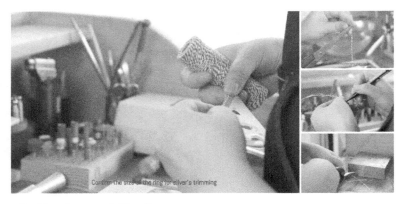

Step 2: Heating and Cooling

Heat the four sections of the silver wires with a heater and soften them.

Use cold water to cool them down.

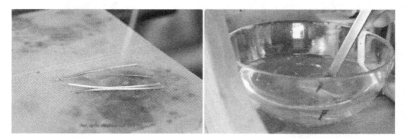

Step 3: The First Pattern

Place one of the silver wires onto the platform and choose the vertical hammer to hammer it with evenly.

The vertical patterns will display on the silver wire.

Step 4: The Second Pattern

Place the second silver wire onto the platform and select the hammer of ripple pattern to hammer the wire uniformly.

The ripple patterns will display on the wire.

Step 5: The Third Pattern

With tweezers, clip the two silver wires together and ensure they are straight.

In your clipping, ensure one of the ends is tight, and the other remaining end is clipped together with a tweezer.

Now, I'm going to turn the tweezers and twist the two wires to achieve the shape.

Next is to put it on the platform and hammer it flat.

Step 6: Welding

The three types of silver wires will be placed together and then welded.

Add some welding powder and then heat them to fuse them.

Use cold water to cool it off.

Step 7: Trimming

Due to the process of hammering, twisting, and welding, the silver wire may have been inhomogeneous in length, and I'm going to use scissors to trim the two ends of the silver wire

Step 8: Silver Ball's Making

Trim off a portion of silver wire and use the heater to heat it to make it melt to be the shape of a ball.

Step 9: Decorating

Add welding powder to the two ends of the welded silver and put the silver ball onto the surface.

Weld the silver Ball to the silver using a heater.

Step 10: Polish the Welded Area

After welding, some dirt leaves on the Jewelry, and I will use tools to polish the dirt.

Step 11: Shaping

Put the silver onto the ring mold and use a soft hammer to hammer the silver shape appropriately.

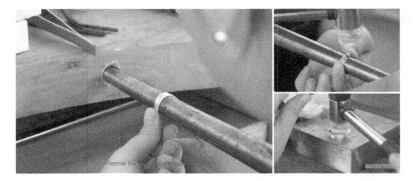

Step 11: Polishing and Cleaning

To clean the ring, place it into the polishing machine.

As soon as you are done cleaning, soak it in clean water.

Step 13: Completed

Display and snap your finished ring

Textured Silver Dust Ring Without Stones

Step 1: Design

Sketch your ring's outline design on the surface of the silver using a marker.

Use a transparent ruler to confirm the length of the ring.

Step 2: Cutting

From the sterling silver with you, trim out the portion you want according to the outlines using your scissors.

Step 3: Hammering

You will discover that the silver piece you cut out is already bending after the picture's trimming.

You have to use a hammer to make it straight again.

Step 4: Heating

To enable the silver to be softened, you have to heat it.

Step 5: Cool Down

- You can use a tweezer to hold it while putting it inside cold water for cooling.

Step 6: Flatten

It would help if you used a press machine to press down the silver; at this time, it is already soft.

Step 7: Manufacturing Texture

Use a texture hammer to textures and decorative patterns on the lengthened and squashed silver.

Step 8: Time to Trim (TTT)

After the pressing, you will notice a difference in the length of the silver.

Due to the reason above, the size of the ring needs to be measured again.

Step 9: Cutting

Following the markings,      trim the silver accordingly.

Step 10: Polish

Polish the cut edges of the silver to make the incision to be smooth.

Step 11: Making the Shape

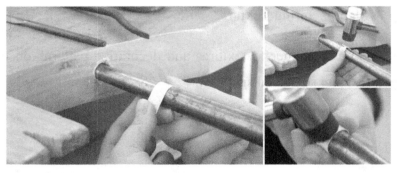

Place the silver onto the ring model.

Bend by applying strength and make it into a ring with an opening.

To make it firm and fixed, you have to hammer it hard.

Step 12: Cutting/Hammering/Polishing

Use another smaller piece of silver and follow the same procedures as shown above.

The essence of this piece is for use in the next step.

Step 13: Combination

Put the small piece of silver above the opening ring and start bending it.

Slightly hammer, as the image shows, to fit these two parts well.

Step 14: Adding Solder Powder

Attach the ring to the table and add some welding powder to the portion where the welding will occur.

Put the smaller piece of silver above.

Step 15: Welding

Join the two ends that need to be welded together and welded utterly.

Step 16: Cool Down

Use a tweezer to place it inside cold water for cooling.

Step 17: Shaping

Place the already welded ring back into the ring model and hammer it gently to fix its shape.

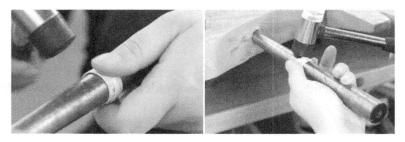

Step 18: Put Inside the Deoxidized Solution

Put the ring into the deoxidized solution and allow it for about 20 minutes.

Step 19: Cleaning Up

Use the brush to remove some dirt from the surface of the ring.

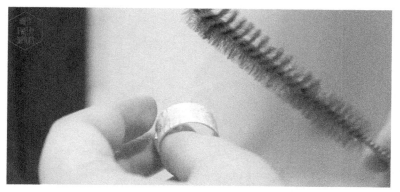

Step 20: Completed Weigh and Display
your ring.

Take a photograph of your ring.

Silver Stacking Rings: Silver Band

Step 1: Cutting and Annealing The Cutting:

The first end square should be filed

Cut with a saw after marking the needed length using a sharpie

The newly cut end square should be filed. Crosscheck the length. If you notice it's too long, file it down to the required size.

The Annealing:

Coat the outside with a thin layer of a fire coat using a small brush.

Position it on a block of charcoal.

Ensure you aneal with a reduced flame.

At this time, quench and pickle the piece.

Neutralize it in a mixture of water/Baking Soda.

Step 2: Forming

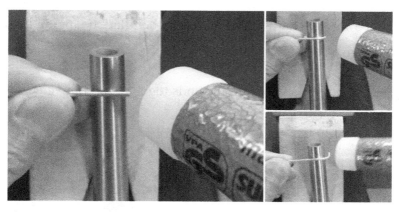

Now that your wire is annealed, it is time to form it into shape.

With a mandrel, put the wire at a smaller diameter than your ring size.

As the wire sticks a bit beyond the point of contact, strike down on end with a nylon-faced dead blow mallet. As soon as that is done, the wire will bend downward.

Make an advance of the wire to 1 or 2mm and keep stroking it until it is nearly curved halfway. Your end shape should be near an oval piece.

With the dead blow mallet, hammer the ends to close the oval. With the oval shape, the soldering will be more comfortable.

Place the ring on a hard flat surface and then flatten tapping it with the full face of the dead blow mallet.

Use needle-nose pliers to pull the ends together or your fingers.

Step 3: Soldering

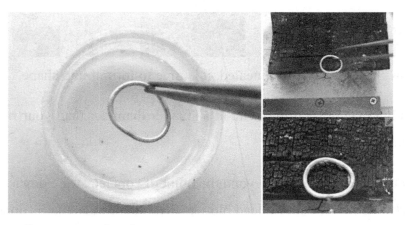

Use a fire coat on the ring.

The coated ring should be placed on the block of charcoal while the seam faces you.

Use a piece of solders and cut out a 1 x 1 mm square from the actual work. It is wise to cut a few extras just in case of shortage. Then position on a block of charcoal.

Put flux to the seam and Solder.

The ring should be heated uniformly using a reducing blue flame. Applying heat to the Solder makes it melt and form a ball.

Quench, pickle, and neutralize, as demonstrated above.

Examine the joint of the seam. If you notice any high or swollen spots from the Solder, you can file lightly or sand.

Step 4: Last Forming and Polishing

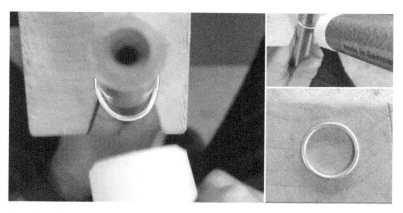

Put the back of the ring onto the ring mandrel.

Use the dead blow mallet to tap down the ring on the high spots lightly.

Make your way around the ring. Then begin to tap in and lightly downward.

This tapping will make the ring take a circular shape.

Be flipping the ring as often as possible because the mandrel has been tapered.

When tapping down the ring to your required size, it should be perfectly round.

Now polish the ring on a buffing wheel, and you are through!

If you want as many stacking rings as possible, repeat these processes.

## Silver Fork Bracelet

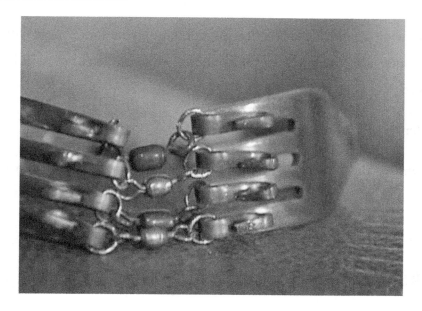

## Step 1

Decide on where the handle of the fork will be cut off from.

Some forks have a natural brake on the handle - either a position where it tapers or a decorative rind or design. In case the fork has one of these, cut off from there.

If not, cut off the handle up an inch lower where it flares out for the tines.

## Step 2

Secure the tine ends of the fork in a vise carefully.

Wearing gloves and safety glasses, cut through the fork handle with a rotary tool fitted with a metal cutting wheel; a hacksaw will be fine.

Step 3

Remove the fork from the vise using a pair of pliers and keep it apart.

You must repeat the process when you want to cut the other fork.

Step 4

keep them in tines down on a heat-resistant platform as soon as both forks have been cut to the average length.

This platform could be a cement board, cement itself, or metal.

Step 5

Use a propane torch to heat the horks for quick and painless metal bending.

Let the flame burn while you hold it at about 2" inches from the silver, and heat until the forks turn cherry red.

Step 6

Allow the forks to cool on their own to room temperature.

Don't be in a hurry by putting them in a cold medium like an ice pack or cold water.

Don't panic even if the metal is discolored; this will be taken care of in other steps.

Step 7

As soon as the metal has cooled down, put the fork in a vise and tines down as the front of the fork faces your direction.

Step 8

Use tongue and groove pliers with tape to protect the silver by covering the slip lock's teeth.

Like the teeth, hold the rest of the fork's handle area using the pliers and bend gently towards your direction to create the bracelet shape.

Gradually make the bend as the metal eases into the required shape.

The fork should be removed from the vise from time to time to ascertain its fitness.

Step 9

The second fork should be bent in the same way.

Step 10

As soon as the forks are bent, place one fork back into the vise so the bend can face out of your direction.

Allow it for about 1" of the tines secured in the vise.

Step 11

Grasp the fork using the tape-wrapped pliers at the bottom of the tines and softly bend the piece towards your direction - to about 90 degrees.

Do the same for the other fork.

Step 12

With needle nose pliers, bend the tines more and create a curl or loop on the tip every time.

Step 13

With a rotary tool having a little wire wheel fixed, you can remove any discoloration caused by the heat.

Step 14

Match jump rings over the forks' curled tines and uses extra jump rings or swivels to link the forks together at the tines.

As soon as you have finished the bracelet, begin to solder the jump rings shut, so the bracelet's weight doesn't separate them.

Step 15

You can also "weave" the tines together instead of using the jump rings.

Keep on sliding the forks together until the curled lines line up.

Now put a single tine cut from another fork.

As soon as you are sure they fit in, remove the single tine, heat it with the propane torch, and allow it to cool naturally.

Then, Slide it back into the curled tines.

Curl every end of the single tine to hold it in position and keep it from snagging on clothing.

Step 16

To link and round up the bracelet's underside, drill a hole at the end of every handle fork.

Add a silver swivel and a jump ring to each hole, then match it with a lobster clasp.

To maintain it even simpler, make the large bends in the fork match your wrist a little tighter and wear it as a cuff bracelet.

Copper and Silver Spinner Ring

Step 1: Measure, Cut, and Prepare

Measure the size of your finger to a tight fit because, during hammering, the ring will extend.

Your desired size should be marked on the copper.

Saw the copper shape and cut the silver wire about 6mm longer than the copper.

Now anneal the metals. It implies heating them with the torch's help until you notice a yellow/orange flame from the metal before the metal becomes reddish.

- Allow cooling.

The essence of annealing is to make the metal softer for bending.

Step 2: Bending the Metal

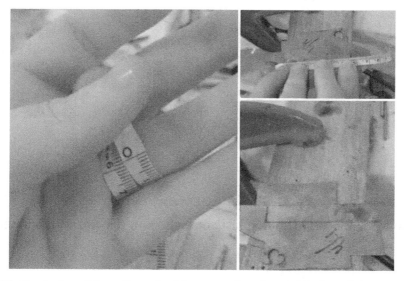

With the help of the pliers, hold one end and quickly bend the metal within so the ends connect. The ends will require adjoining perfectly without gaps, so you may need to see it straight.

You will notice from one of the pics that as soon as you are done with the ring, the saw will project forward, and those saw blades are very sharp.

To ensure a tight join, overlap the ends first and carefully pull them asunder enough to join them flush; that way, the pressure is still ready to push both ends together.

Step 3: Solder and Size

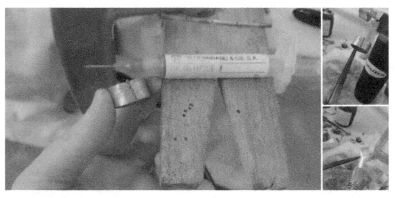

Run a small bead of solder paste onto the join (ensure you maintain a clean and friendly metal).

Place the ring onto the solder brick and heat the metal with your torch.

Spreading the heat around but focusing mainly on the opposite side of your joint is the best way to solder.

Observe the Solder kingly, and when your entire piece is bright red, your Solder will melt in a little second.

Immediately, you notice that removing the heat as your Solder will keep running around the ring and out of the join, which will be useful.

Switch off the ring or keep it cool on the brick.

Step 4: Smoothen Off

Sand out any extra solder if required, and then put the ring onto the mandrel. With your hammer, hammer the ring all through, taking off the ring and flipping it over each side as often as possible.

You would want to shape it at this point, so focus on your progress.

As soon as the copper ring is round, the silver spinner is Solder, and repeat the process of hammering it all through. You could also include a hammered effect to the spinner by using the hammer's ball-peen end to dent it.

Step 5: The Fine Tuning

Please put on the ring to ensure it matches your finger. If not, continue hammering on the mandrel until you have stretched it enough.

As soon as it matches, sand it slightly, that is, if the rough look is not severe, and then check the spinner ring size.

You need to stretch this one out until it's more significant than the copper ring so it can get still within it.

Step 6: Flare and Finish

Use sandpaper to sand the edges and all portions required; make it up to your taste.

Position the ring on an excellent surface and use the ball of part of the hammer to match the ring's center.

Hit the hammer to create a flare on the edge of the ring. Be careful and move slowly, as more flare could occur on one side, not the other.

The spinner won't come off the flared end as soon as you are satisfied. Put the spinner onto the ring and complete the flare of the other side of the ring, trapping it inside the spinner.

Polish the ring a little and round it up.

Heart-Shaped Lock

Step 1: Cutting and Building Your Mold

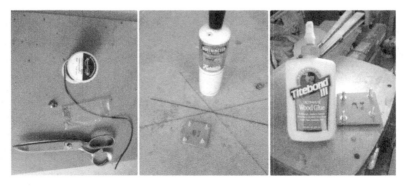

Make a sketch drawing of your required shape on top of the wood, then drill and cut it off with a scroll saw.

You may wish to glue, clamp, or bolt the two parts of the mold together. Molds of this kind are always suitable for one casting.

Step 2: Heating and Casting Your metal

You can make your casting medium nice and "liquidy" while using your torch; ensure you take precautions! Put on your gloves and face masks to avoid inhalation. Keep water nearby in case of a fire outbreak.

Pour gently and uniformly; I cast my many times. The reason was that there was much silver in the mold, or maybe not much! As much as possible, do not put water on the cast; allow it to cool gradually.

Step 3: Polishing the Rough Casting

Once you are satisfied with the cast, file up to any rough parts and include pretty details.

Move it to a polishing wheel and make it a shiny finish. It takes up to 15 minutes to achieve this.

Step 4: String Up

You can use a chain, leather, or line for the string and round up the necklace.

Step 5: Sizing Your Pretty Necklace

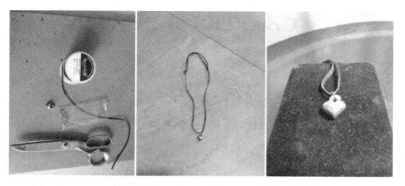

I gave this pretty necklace to my wife, and it's nice on her; she was delighted with the look.

# CHAPTER SEVEN

## HEALTH AND SAFETY MEASURES: MACHINERY, CHEMICAL, HEATING, AND SOLDERING

Machinery

Safety Measures When Using Metalworking Machine

Read the owner's manuals carefully because metalworking machines can be dangerous if not correctly used.

Ensure you receive instructions and proper training before using any tool or machine.

Inspect and adjust all safety gear before each job.

Ensure that the guards are in position and in good working condition before operating.

Ensure all stationery equipment is anchored securely to the floor or table.

Ensure all machines have an emergency stop button (e-stop).

Ensure all machines have a start/stop button within easy reach of the operator.

Ensure you know correctly how to stop the machine during an emergency.

Ensure all cutting tools and blades are clean and sharp. They should be able to cut smoothly without applying force.

Stop the machine before measuring, cleaning, or making any adjustments.

Perform appropriate lockout steps before starting maintenance or repairs.

Clean machines, dust, hoods, and other areas if there is the possibility of a combustible dust situation.

Ensure there is enough room around the machine to do the job safely.

Clean all tools after use.

Return all portable tooling to its proper storage place after use.

Keep your hands away from the cutting head and all moving components.

Chemical

Avoid Toxic Fumes:

A benchtop fume extractor may be necessary here to remove harmful fumes caused by soldering and flux from the soldering workshop by filtering the air.

Work in a well-ventilated area. The smoke formed is mainly from the flux and could irritate and aggravate asthma.

Avoid breathing it by keeping your head to the side of, not above, your work. Dangers of Exposure to Lead:

Lead present on your skin can be ingested, and lead fumes can be given off during soldering.

Other metal fumes are likely pollutants and hazardous to the human system.

Lead can have severe chronic health implications, such as respiratory, digestive, and nerve disorders, memory and concentration problems, and muscle and joint pain.

Heating

Heating Precautions:

When heated sterling silver, care must be taken to avoid "overheating."

In torch heating, it is essential to see that no part of the work is overheated and that all parts of the object or article are brought to the full heating temperature. Since sterling silver heats so rapidly, it is unnecessary to hold it at the heating temperature for too long.

A closed furnace has certain advantages; since the object's temperature can be more precisely controlled, the heat can be absorbed more evenly.

However, the heating time must be established by trial and error for articles of different sizes and shape-and for other size furnaces.

It is preferable to heat silver alloys in a neutral or reducing atmosphere to prevent the formation of copper oxides.

The right heating temperature for normal softening of sterling silver is between 1100F and 12000F. Temperatures above 1200F(649C.) tend to dissolve the copper-rich phase, and unless the cooling rate is rigidly controlled, the maximum softness will not be achieved.

Soldering

Iron Safety:

Never touch the element or tip of the soldering iron. They are very hot, up to 400°C, and it burns.

Ensure the cleaning sponge is wet when in use.

Turn the unit off or unplug it when not in use.

Always return the soldering iron to its stand when not in use.

Hold wires to be heated with tweezers or clamps.


Work Safety with Solder:

- Use lead-free Solder.

- Wear eye protection because Solder can "spit."

- Always wash your hands with soap and water after soldering.

# CHAPTER EIGHT

## HOW TO SELL YOUR JEWELRY ART

We shall look at eight easy steps to successfully selling your jewelry art online since the world is a global community.

Table of Content:

1. Thinking About Your Niche

2. Determine Where You Would Want to Sell

3. Making Up Your Store

4. Displaying Your Products

5. Putting Price Tags and Setting Up Payments

6. Setting Up Shipping

7. Promoting Your Products

8. Managing Your Stock

1. Thinking About Your Niche

- The first thing to consider when selling anything online is your niche - and the same is applicable when selling Jewelry.

You have to answer these questions below:

- Who are my potential buyers?

- Where will the customers shop from?

- How can I meet my clients?

To answer the questions, let's go this way; it's important to understand what you are selling and who you are selling to. Knowing this will help you in the following steps; for instance, it will give you a better idea of which platform to sell on and what branding choices are most suitable to catch your audience's attention. If your handmaking Jewelry is for young people, for instance, you can decide to sell them on social media and use it as a fun, light tone for your branding. But if it's engagement rings, you might wish to launch it on a more professional website to display your Jewelry.

Your niche has a significant impact on your selling adventure. But before forging ahead, ensure you have these at the back of your mind:

- Examine the Jewelry you are selling very well

- Give a thought about who might want to buy your Jewelry

- Think about possible ways of reaching your audience.

2. Determine Where You Would Want to Sell (Online)

The right place to sell your Jewelry online depends on your needs, goals, and audience, so we begin to think about these three things as we move along. Examples of places you can make use of online are:

- Social media - like Facebook and Instagram

- Online marketplaces - like eBay, Amazon, and Etsy

- Your online store - which can be built using a platform like Square Online

The advantages of each of these platforms will be highlighted below:

- Social media: is best for hobbyists who are selling a small range of products

• Online marketplace: is best for quickly getting your products in front of a large customer base • Online store: is best for professional sellers or starters

Before forging ahead, ensure you have the following:

• Looked at the selling platforms listed above

• Give a thought about whether you would want to combine multiple selling channels

• Determine the one you are going for

3. Making Up Your Store

As soon as you choose where to sell your products online, you must make up things in your store and get them ready to be at your customer's doorstep. There's an easy setup for any of the channels you choose!

1. Social media: selling on social media can be a bit fiddly to set up, and it varies a lot from one platform to the other. You can check out our specific guides to creating a social media seller account.

Setting Up Facebook Shopping Page: To create a Facebook shopping page, you have to be the admin of your business page, sell physical products, and accept Facebook terms and conditions. Only this way you could create an actual Facebook shopping center.

Enable Facebook Shops:

- Set up an account with Facebook's commerce manager

- Create a collection

- Customize your storefront

- Publish your shop

Setting Up a Business Instagram Account:

- From your settings, switch to a business profile, then sync your Facebook store (or online store) with your Instagram account to pull your products into your Instagram account.

Begin to Create Content: as soon as you have set up your store, you need to upload photos - then go to post settings and start selecting Tag products. It will enable your followers to locate and buy the products they love from your feed. Start creating posts, share them with your story, use hashtags, and connect with influencers to promote your products. Ensure the Shop tab is activated in your Instagram profile.

E-commerce Builders: This platform is the easiest way to create your online store. With this, there is no need for coding or hiring an expensive developer. The process is straightforward: Choose a template, customize it, add your products, tailor your settings, choose a domain name, and publish.

Choosing an E-commerce Builder: you can choose any of the websites listed below for your jewelry art selling: Square Online, BigCommerce, Squarespace, Wix eCommerce, etc.

Square Online is the builder most recommended to most jewelry sellers.

4. Displaying Your Products

Below are the top tips on displaying your products to attract customers' attention.

Customizing Your Store: How you design the front of your store sends similar messages to online customers. An adequately designed storefront can raise customers' trust and help show off your products simultaneously.

Writing a Captivating Description: With an online store, you can never observe which item, in particular, the customer is admiring - you can't stroll down over and use your excellent sales skills to woo them into making a purchase. But what you can do, is write an enticing, persuasive, and informative product description.

Take High-Quality Images: those excellent descriptions won't be enough to persuade people to click that buy button. People want to see the quality of what they are going for, so you need to take professional photos of your products. 5. Putting Price Tags and Setting Up Payments

1. Always cover your costs: at the bare minimum, you need to ensure you are not selling at a loss.

2. Research the market: Look for similar jewelry sellers like you and look at their prices. Find out why they could charge that much, and then compare your product's price with theirs.

3. Apply this formula: Total cost of product + Markup % = Final Product Price.

4. Ensure you set consistent pricing across your products and are clear enough for customers to view them, like the picture below.

5b. Settle Up Payments

The significant thing here is to connect your account to your store so customers' payments can go directly into your bank account.

Payment Gateway: below is a quick list of the leading payment options available.

• Square

• Apple Pay

• Amazon Pay

• PayPal

• Stripe

There are other payment options, like manual payment and wire transfers. Etsy has two options - Payments or PayPal. Square Online is ideal if you have a brick-and-mortar or pop-up shop store that uses a square to accept payments.

Check Transaction Fees: Some e-commerce builders charge transaction fees, while others, like BigCommerce, Wix, and Squarespace, do not. For instance, Etsy charges a transaction fee of 5%, while Amazon charges a "referral fee" for each item you feel - the fee varies depending on the category.

For Jewelry, Amazon's referral fee is 20% for the portion of the total sales price up to $250 and 5% for any amount greater than $250. But the minimum referral fee is $0.30.

6. Promoting Your Jewelry Products Online

You can do your store a massive favor by getting on top of these five things: email marketing, social media, multichannel selling, SEO, and customer reviews.

Email Marketing:

Email marketing remains one of the most effective ways of reaching your customers. You can promote new products, announce sales and discounts, release blog updates, or send out personalized suggestions when you send out emails.

Social Media:

One of the great ways of promoting your brand is through social media. Even if you don't sell through social media, it is still a fantastic way of helping new customers discover your Jewelry and reengage existing customers. You can share photos of different customers wearing your Jewelry and even run competitions to help build your brand and online audience.

Multichannel Selling:

Multichannel selling provides many easy sell options within different platforms, such as Amazon, eBay, Facebook, and Instagram. BigCommerce is the top point when it comes to multichannel selling. All sales can easily be managed from one place with Big e-commerce's built-in integrations.

SEO:

SEO means (Search Engine Optimization). It makes your website visible in search engines such as Google, Bing, and more. E-commerce website builders have built-in SEO tools that automatically make search engines pay attention. However, you can still do other

Things to optimize your website and help your store to rank more highly in Google.

Shopify, BigCommerce, Squarespace, and Wix all have SEO guides and tools to help you achieve this.

Customer Reviews:

Customer reviews come with a lot of power: about 95% of customers read online reviews before purchasing. They are somehow out of your control, but do not worry about this - they can be a helpful tool for building customer trust and boosting sales. If the Jewelry you are selling is costly, then customer trust is crucial for achieving success, and this is where reviews come to play. Ensure you publish both bad and good reviews online - the trick is to respond positively to both as much as possible.

Reviews are especially vital, mostly when selling on marketplaces like Amazon. Positive star ratings and reviews feed into Amazon's algorithm - so the better you do, the higher you are likely to rank in Amazon's search results.

Before you progress, ensure you have the following:

- Created an email marketing campaign and put it into action.

- Optimize your store for SEO to help it rank in search results.

- Set up multichannel selling to include at least one other platform.

- Started gathering customer reviews.

- Created a professional social media account.

7. Managing Your Stock

It is where an e-commerce website builder can perform better, all thanks to inventory tracking. This inventory tracking helps you manage your orders and track stock levels - it is vital to avoid selling the same product twice or missing orders from customers. By following your inventory for you, builders such as Square Online can monitor stock levels, alerts you when stock is out or low, and even automatically label products on-site as "Out of Stock" or "Low Stock."

Square Online, Squarespace, and Big Commerce are top choices when discussing inventory tracking. They got it all - not only can they track your inventory for you, but they can also give you revenue reports and inform you how many customers have visited your site.

Before moving on as an online seller, ensure you have the following:

- Set up inventory tracking for your store.

- Set up a way to mark low and out-of-stock items on your storefront.

# CONCLUSION

Silver metal comes in either wire or flat sheets. These are cut, shaped, soldered, and polished into pieces of Jewelry via silversmithing techniques. To achieve silversmithing jewelry, a silversmith needs to pass through the following techniques: sawing/cutting, filing, hammering, shaping, soldering, finishing and polishing, etc.

There is no doubt that jewelry silversmithing is an excellent technique to learn if you want to climb higher in designing your silver jewelry. As a beginner, you need patients, but with time, you will arrive there.

**OTHER BOOKS BY THE AUTHOR:**

**BLADESMITHING FOR BEGINNERS:** Easy

Step by Step Guide on How to Forge Knives and

Handles.

Made in the USA
Monee, IL
28 November 2023

47549214R00056